JA-PURR-NESE

Adorable Cat-shaped Recipes from Sushi to Soup

LAURE KIÉ & HARUNA KISHI

MITCHELL BEAZLEY

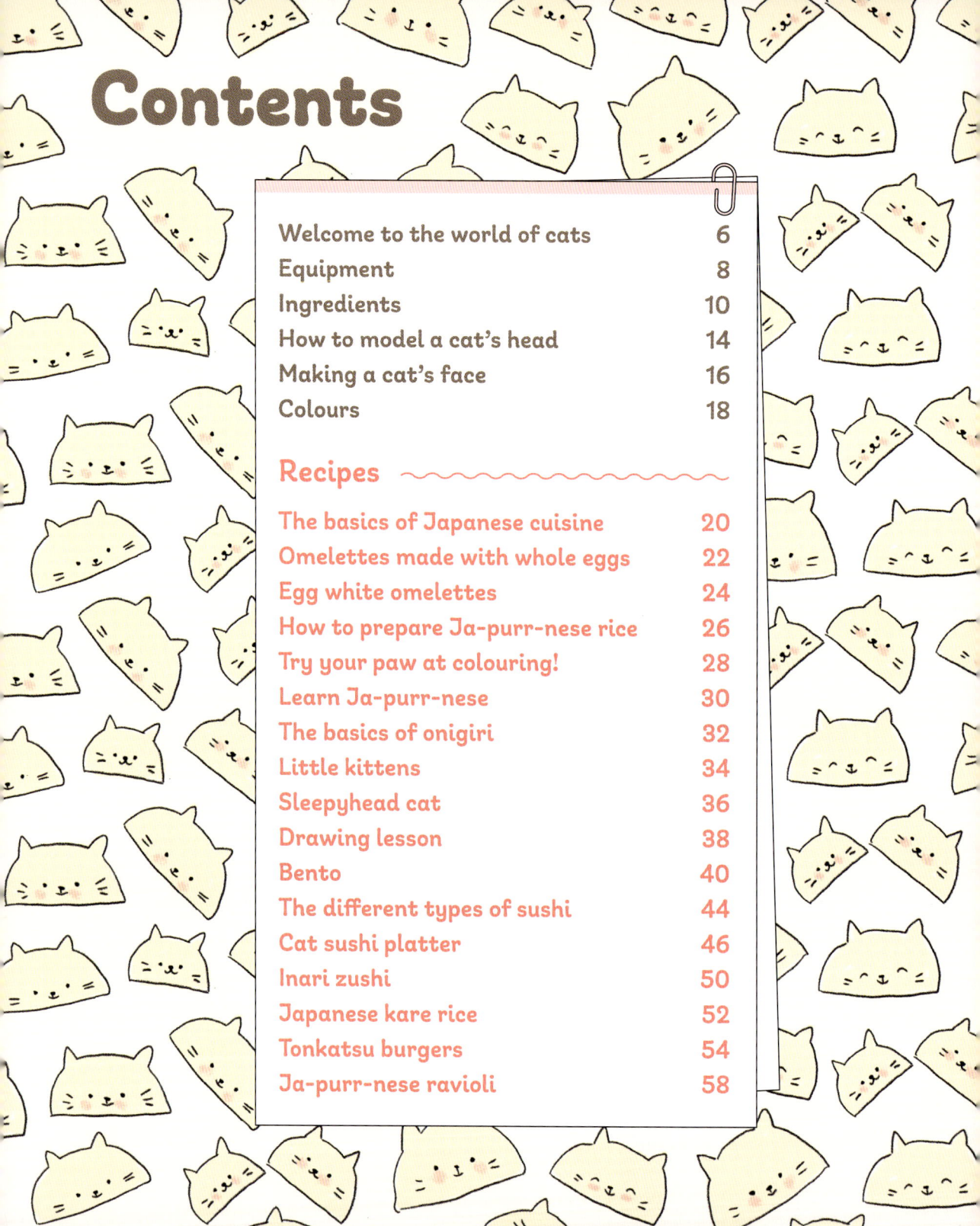

Contents

Welcome to the world of cats — 6
Equipment — 8
Ingredients — 10
How to model a cat's head — 14
Making a cat's face — 16
Colours — 18

Recipes

The basics of Japanese cuisine — 20
Omelettes made with whole eggs — 22
Egg white omelettes — 24
How to prepare Ja-purr-nese rice — 26
Try your paw at colouring! — 28
Learn Ja-purr-nese — 30
The basics of onigiri — 32
Little kittens — 34
Sleepyhead cat — 36
Drawing lesson — 38
Bento — 40
The different types of sushi — 44
Cat sushi platter — 46
Inari zushi — 50
Japanese kare rice — 52
Tonkatsu burgers — 54
Ja-purr-nese ravioli — 58

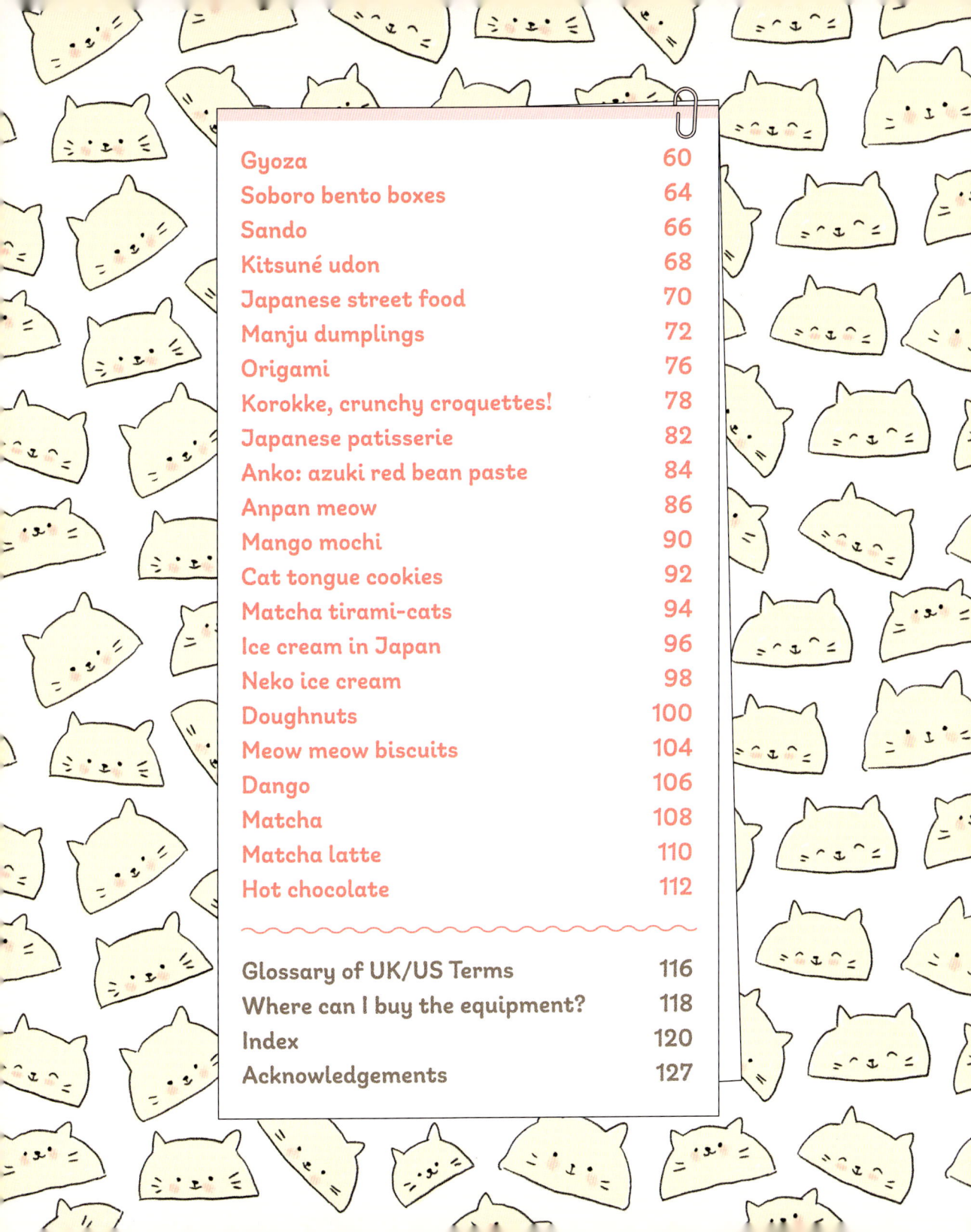

Gyoza	60
Soboro bento boxes	64
Sando	66
Kitsuné udon	68
Japanese street food	70
Manju dumplings	72
Origami	76
Korokke, crunchy croquettes!	78
Japanese patisserie	82
Anko: azuki red bean paste	84
Anpan meow	86
Mango mochi	90
Cat tongue cookies	92
Matcha tirami-cats	94
Ice cream in Japan	96
Neko ice cream	98
Doughnuts	100
Meow meow biscuits	104
Dango	106
Matcha	108
Matcha latte	110
Hot chocolate	112
Glossary of UK/US Terms	116
Where can I buy the equipment?	118
Index	120
Acknowledgements	127

Welcome to the world of cats

Cats hold a very special place in Japanese culture. Above all, they are much-loved, lifelong companions but they also embody powerful symbols in the collective imagination.

One such example is Maneki-neko (neko means 'cat' in Japanese), the bringer of good fortune. Like a lucky charm, it is frequently seen at the entrance to shops or restaurants, a raised paw beckoning customers to enter as doing so will bring them good luck.

Many of us are lucky enough to experience the calm and solace that a cat can bring. Who could fail to be tempted by a dish created to appeal both visually and to the taste buds?

My intention in writing this book is to bring together two warm and comforting worlds, those of Japanese cuisine and small felines.

Thanks to the skill and fine detail of Rennie's photographs and Haruna's kawaii ('adorable' in English) illustrations, cats come to life in this book as onigiri, korokke, mochi or even a matcha latte, and the recipes taste as gorgeous as they look.

Welcome to a world full of the sweetness and cuteness of cats. Meow!

Laure Kié

Equipment

What you need to make cats that are super kawaii!

Tweezers

Scissors, scalpel or a craft knife and a sugarcraft modelling tool

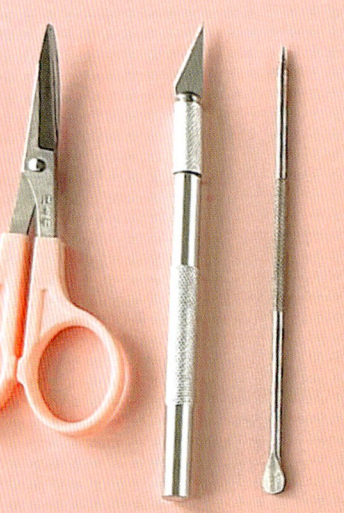

Stencils

Punches

Piping bag

Cutters

Rice moulds

See page 118 for where to buy equipment.

Ingredients

Matcha: green tea powder

Rice vinegar

Tonkatsu sauce

Dashi: sachet of Japanese stock

Japanese rice

Panko: Japanese dried breadcrumbs

Miso

Nori: maki seaweed sheets

Soy sauce

Toasted sesame oil

Udon: thick wheat flour noodles

Golden (blond) sesame seeds

Japanese curry spice mix: powdered or cubes

Anko: azuki red bean paste

Inari: fried tofu pouches

Ingredients

Japanese rice

Japonica is a variety of round-grain rice with a high starch content, which gives it a slightly sticky texture. It is ideal for picking up with chopsticks or for making onigiri rice balls.

Nori

The most widely eaten seaweed as it is used to make the famous maki rolls. Sold in sheets, it is eaten as is, but care should be taken not to get the sheets wet.

Toasted sesame oil

This very aromatic oil is extracted from roasted sesame seeds. It is used to season salads and also to add flavour to a stew or to raw fish. To be used sparingly.

White (blond) sesame seeds

Sesame plays an important part in Japanese cuisine, in the form of an oil, as seeds or as a paste. The seeds are often lightly crushed in a pestle and mortar to extract more flavour. They are combined with salt in gomashio to season onigiri.

Soy sauce

Made from soy beans, wheat, water and salt, this sauce is an essential ingredient in Japanese cuisine. It is the equivalent of salt in western cuisines.

Rice vinegar

This very mild vinegar is made by fermenting rice. In Japanese cuisine, it is an essential ingredient for seasoning salads, making pickled vegetables and in the preparation of sushi rice (page 46).

Tonkatsu sauce
A thick, vegetable- and fruit-based sauce that is served as an accompaniment to deep-fried dishes such as korokke (page 78), or a tonkatsu burger (page 54).

Inari
Pouches of fried tofu that have been seasoned and simmered for a long time in a richly flavoured sauce. Used for making inari zushi (page 50) or kitsuné udon (page 68).

Miso
This fermented paste is made from soy beans and rice or barley. Used daily in Japan, mainly in the soup of the same name.

Udon
Made from wheat flour, salt and water, udon noodles are white and vary in size according to the region where they are made. Sold dried or fresh, they can be added to soups, stocks (page 68) or a cold dish.

Panko
Breadcrumbs made from sandwich bread that, when fried, become very crisp. They are used to coat korokke croquettes (page 78) or tonkatsu (page 54).

Japanese kare
Cubes made from an Indian curry spice roux (a thickening agent) that dissolve in meat or vegetable cooking liquids. They are used to prepare Japanese kare rice (page 52).

Dashi
This stock is a basic ingredient of Japanese cuisine. It can be bought in powder form or made at home, its main ingredients being seaweed and dried fish.

Matcha
Matcha is green tea in powdered form and is used in Japanese tea ceremonies. It has also become a staple ingredient in Japanese cakes and pastries.

Anko
This sweet red paste made from azuki beans is similar to chestnut purée and it forms the base of a great many traditional pastries. See the recipe on page 84.

How to model a cat's head

Whether made from small balls of rice, brioche or ordinary bread dough, sweet little cats' heads can be cut out or moulded for use in various dishes, each more fun than the last.

The basic shape

This shape works for both 'flat' foods (like cookies) or those that are small and ball-shaped.

1 Draw or shape the rice or dough into a slightly round oval.

2 Add 2 tiny triangles for the ears (not too pointed).

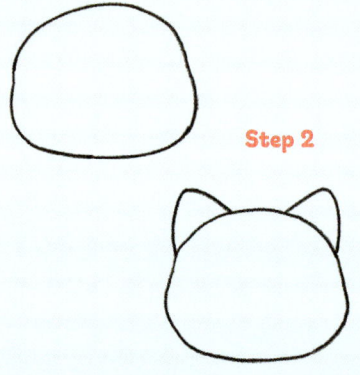

Step 2

For bases made of bread, brioche (for making anpan) or mashed potato (for making korokke)

1 Shape the bread or mashed potato into slightly round but oval-shaped small balls.

2 Shape the ears:

- either by forming separate triangles and sticking 2 on top of each ball
- or by pinching the top of each ball with 2 fingers.

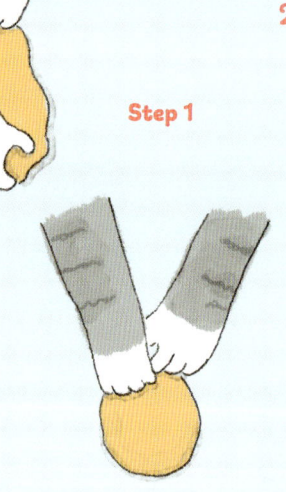

Step 1

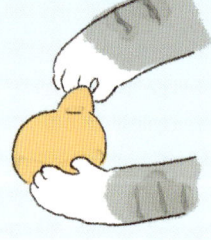

Step 2

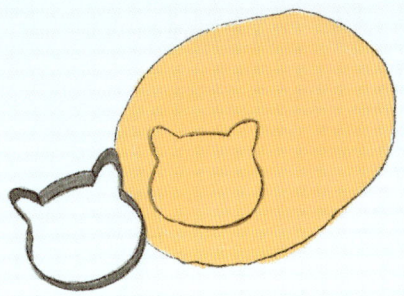

For making onigiri

Follow the steps on page 32.

For thin bases…

such as cookies, slices of sandwich bread, crêpes made with egg, cheese, ham, etc., use a shaped cutter (page 9) which can also serve as a stencil.

For making layered dishes…

such as matcha tiramisu (page 94) or a sandwich (page 66), use a mould in the shape of a cat's head (page 9) or a large pastry cutter.

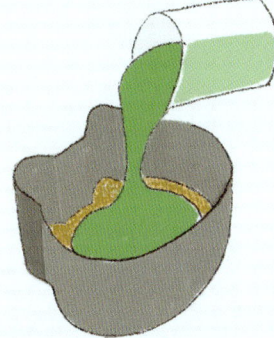

Making a cat's face

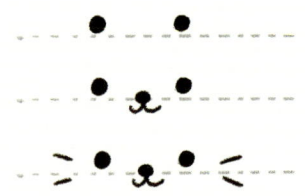

The basics: create the different features of the face in three steps

1 Start with the eyes.

2 Place the muzzle in the centre, on the line below the eyes.

3 Finish with 2 lines on each side for whiskers, level with the line of the muzzle.

For savoury recipes

Face outline cut from nori seaweed (for onigiri)

Step 1

Step 2

1 Using a nori punch, cut out the eyes and muzzle (a classic punch can also be used for the eyes and scissors for the muzzle).

2 Using scissors, cut 4 thin strips about 1.5cm (⅝ inch) long, for whiskers.

3 Using tweezers, position the eyes, muzzle and whiskers on the cut-out face.

The finishing touches

If the steps described above have resulted in a recognizable cat's face, add the finishing touches as follows:

1 Ears made from ham.

2 A muzzle made from cheese (very useful if the base of the face is dark since, if it is, the nori will not stand out enough).

3 Cheekbones made from ketchup.

Step 3

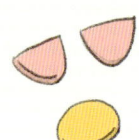

For sweet recipes

Use a simple DIY baking parchment piping cone filled with melted chocolate (dark or milk) to outline a cat's features for almost all sweet recipes.

How to make a baking parchment cone for piping chocolate

1 Cut a triangle of baking parchment.

2 Roll point C towards point A to make a cone.

3 Do the same with point B.

4 Lightly fold over points A, B and C to stop the cone unrolling and stand it point down in a tall glass.

5 Melt squares of chocolate in a bain-marie (a heatproof bowl over a pan of simmering water), spoon the melted chocolate into the cone and fold over the open end to enclose the chocolate.

6 Snip off the tip of the cone with scissors (take care not to cut off too much to begin with, cut just a little, test and then cut off more if necessary).

Drawing the face of the cat

1 Begin by piping 2 dots for the eyes.

2 Pipe the muzzle between the eyes.

3 On the same horizontal line, pipe 2 thin lines on each side for whiskers. Leave the chocolate to set.

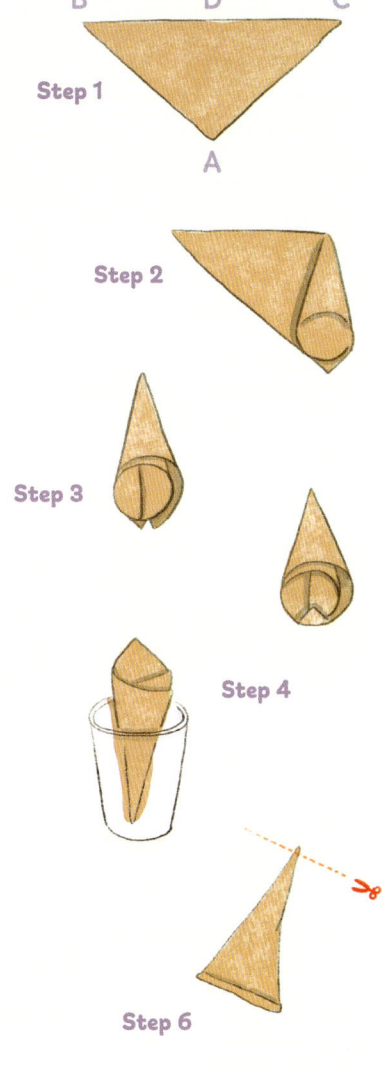

Colours

To create a dish that appeals both to the eyes and the taste buds, use a wide range of different colours. To find the right balance, choose from this list of different foods classified by colour group.

Chestnut brown/brown
- Plain dark chocolate
- Brown sugar
- Soy sauce
- Kinako (roasted soy bean flour)
- White (blond) sesame seeds
- Brown miso
- Chopped cooked beef
- Fried tofu
- Katsuobushi (bonito flakes)

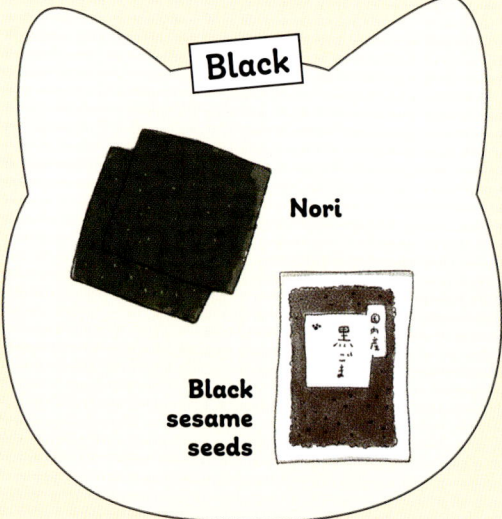

Black
- Nori
- Black sesame seeds

Yellow
- Egg yolk
- Sweetcorn kernels

The basics of Japanese cuisine

To start making Japanese dishes, there are only a few basic techniques to master, such as how to prepare the famous Ja-purr-nese rice. The instructions on the pages that follow will give you all the tools you need to cook perfect rice and egg omelettes.

Omelettes made with whole eggs

Makes 2 omelettes
Prep time: 2 minutes
Cooking time: 3 minutes

Ingredients

- 2 eggs
- pinch of salt
- drizzle of vegetable oil

1 Beat the eggs and salt together in a bowl.

2 Heat the oil in a non-stick frying pan, then pour in half the beaten egg mixture, swirling the pan so it coats the base in a thin, even layer.

3 Leave to cook for 1–2 minutes.

4 Turn the omelette over and cook it for a few more seconds.

5 Remove the omelette from the pan and make a second one in the same way using the remaining beaten egg mixture.

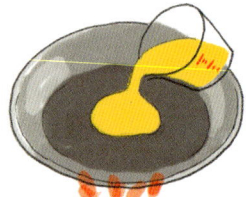
Step 2

Step 4

Step 1

Uses

1 As a semicircle: spoon your chosen filling over one half of the omelette and fold the other half over as a cover.

2 As a rectangle: place the omelette on a board and cut off 2 opposing sides to make a roughly rectangular shape, which is more suited to bento boxes, for example.

Step 2

Egg white omelettes

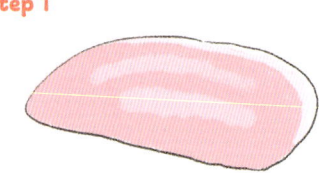

Step 1

Makes 2 omelettes
Prep time: 2 minutes
Cooking time: 3 minutes

Ingredients

- 1 slice of cooked ham
- 2 eggs
- pinch of salt
- drizzle of vegetable oil

1 Using a small decorative cutter, cut out shapes (such as flowers, hearts or stars) from the slice of ham.

2 Separate the eggs, putting the egg whites in a mixing bowl (saving the yolks to use in another recipe). Whisk the egg whites with the salt to mix.

3 Heat the oil in a tamagoyaki (rectangular) frying pan, add half the ham shapes, then pour in half the beaten egg white mixture, tilting the pan so it is coated in a thin, even layer.

4 Leave to cook for 1 minute, turn the omelette over and cook it for a few more seconds. Remove the omelette from the pan and make a second one in the same way using the remaining beaten egg mixture.

Step 2

Step 3

Step 4

TIP
An attractive way to serve these is to cut heart shapes out of the egg white omelettes using a small cutter and layer them on top of the whole egg omelettes.

How to prepare Ja-purr-nese rice

Makes 4 large bowls (740g/1lb 10oz cooked rice)
Prep time: 5 minutes
Cooking time: 30 minutes
Resting time: 10 minutes

Ingredients
- 450g (1lb) Japanese rice
- 600ml (20fl oz) water

1 Rinse the rice in several changes of cold water until the water runs clear.

2 Drain the rice and put it into a rice cooker with the water.

3 Cook for the required time and then leave the rice to rest for at least 10 minutes.

Turn to page 46 for sushi rice.

TIP
If you cook the rice in a saucepan, rinse it as for Step 1 above, then drain and put in a saucepan with the water. Bring to the boil, then reduce the heat to very low and cook for 12 minutes. Remove the pan from the heat, cover and leave to rest for about 10 minutes for perfectly fluffy rice.

Try your paw at colouring!

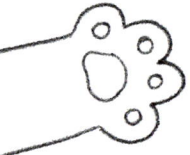
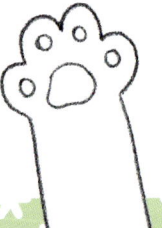

Hello
Konnichiwa
こんにちは

It's good
Oishii desu
おいしいです

Thank you
Arigatō
ありがとう

How are you?
Ogenki desuka?
お元気ですか?

Goodbye
Sayonara
さようなら

Adorable
Kawaii
かわいい

Enjoy your meal/
Bon appetit!
Itadakimasu
いただきます

Hello
Konnichiwa
こんにちは

Adorable
Kawaii
かわいい

Thank you
Arigatō
ありがとう

How are you?
Ogenki desuka?
お元気ですか?

Hello
Konnichiwa
こんにちは

It's good
Oishii desu
おいしいです

Thank you
Arigatō
ありがとう

How are you?
Ogenki desuka?
元気ですか?
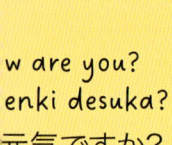

Goodbye
Sayonara
さようなら

Adorable
Kawaii
かわいい

Chopsticks
Ohashi
お箸

Cheers!
Kanpaï !
乾杯

Please
Onegai shimasu
お願いします

Meal
Shokuji
食事

Lunch
Hiru gohan
昼ご飯

Dessert
Dezâto
デザート

Rice
Gohan
デザート

Tea
Ocha
お茶

Please
Onegai shimasu
お願いします

Meal
Shokuji
食事

Lunch
Hiru gohan
昼ご飯

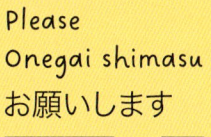

Tea
Ocha
お茶

Dessert
Dezâto
デザート

R
G
ラ

Please
Onegai shimasu
お願いします

Meal
Shokuji
食事

Lunch
Hiru gohan
昼ご飯

The basics of onigiri

Step 1

Step 2

Step 3

How to shape an onigiri cat

1 Dampen your hands and dust them lightly with salt.

2 Using a wooden spoon, scoop up the amount of cooked rice you need.

3 Place your chosen filling in the centre of the rice and press the grains lightly together to make an oval. Next, shape 2 small triangles for ears.

4 Cut the features for the face from a sheet of nori seaweed: 2 eyes, very fine whiskers, a muzzle and 2 small triangles to place inside the ears (optional).

5 Position all the cut pieces of seaweed on your onigiri cat.

Step 4

Step 5

> **TIP**
> Roll the ball continuously between the palms of your hands, applying even pressure so the rice sticks together but avoid compressing it too firmly so as not to crush the grains.

Little kittens

Serves 4
Prep time: 35 minutes
No cooking, apart from the rice

Ingredients

• 4 bowls of hot cooked rice (see instructions for cooking rice, page 26)
• ¼ slice of cooked ham
• 4 thin slices of carrot
• 1 slice of burger cheese
• 1 sheet of nori seaweed
• 1½ tablespoons black sesame seeds
• salt

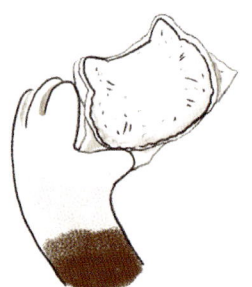

In a mixing bowl, gently stir 4 pinches of salt into the hot rice.
Cut 8 small rounds from the ham for cheeks.
Using a small cutter or a pointed knife, cut flower shapes from the carrot slices.
Cut 4 ovals from the cheese slices for muzzles.
Cut eyes, muzzles and whiskers to make 8 faces, following the instructions on page 16.

White cat

Shape 4 cat heads from the rice, following the instructions on page 32. Cut out eyes, a muzzle and whiskers from the sheet of nori seaweed and position them on the heads, along with the ham cheeks and a carrot flower.
Place 1 teaspoon of salted rice on a piece of clingfilm, then wrap the film around the rice, pressing to compact it into a small ball. Remove the clingfilm. Shape 9 more small balls in the same way.
Cut paw pads from the ham and position these on the paws.

Cat paws

Place 1 tablespoon of salted rice on a piece of clingfilm, then wrap the film around the rice, pressing to compact it into a small ball. Remove the film. Shape 11 more small balls in the same way.
Cut paw pads from nori seaweed and position these on the paws.

Black cat

Crush the sesame seeds in a pestle and mortar and gently mix them into the rest of the salted rice. Shape 4 cat heads following the instructions described on page 32.
Position the eyes, muzzle (cheese plus nori seaweed) and whiskers cut from nori seaweed on each rice ball.
Cut the remaining nori seaweed into fine strips and position on top of each head as tabby markings in the cats' fur.

Sleepyhead cat

**Serves 4
Prep time: 35 minutes
No cooking, apart from the rice and the whole egg omelettes**

Ingredients

- 4 slices of cooked ham
- 2 strips of nori seaweed
- 4 bowls of hot cooked rice (see instructions for cooking rice, page 26)
- 4 large lettuce leaves
- 4 rectangular whole egg omelettes (see recipe, page 22)
- soy sauce
- 10 cherry tomatoes, halved
- salt

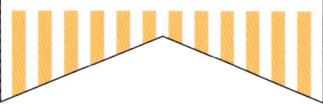

1 Cut 2 small triangles (for ears) from 1 slice of ham, then cut the rest of the ham slice into fine, long strips for the 'ball of wool'.

2 Cut 16 fine strips, 1cm (½ inch) long, from the nori seaweed for whiskers, also 8 rounds for the eyes and 4 for the muzzle.

3 In a mixing bowl, gently stir 4 pinches of salt into the hot rice.

4 Shape 1 cat head following the instructions on page 32. With damp hands, spoon a small amount of rice into the palm of one hand then, pressing lightly, roll the rice between your palms to shape it into a small oval ball to make one paw. Make a second small oval ball for the other paw.

5 Place 1 lettuce leaf on a serving plate. Position the head on the upper part of the lettuce leaf and cover the lower part with 1 rectangular omelette for the bed cover. Next, position the 2 cat's paws.

6 Using a small brush dipped in soy sauce, dab some areas of the face and paws of the cat to represent markings in its fur. Add the nori seaweed eyes, muzzle and whiskers, plus triangles of ham for the ears.

7 Add the ham ball of wool and decorate with the cherry tomatoes.

8 Make 3 more sleepyhead cats in the same way.

Step 6

Drawing lesson

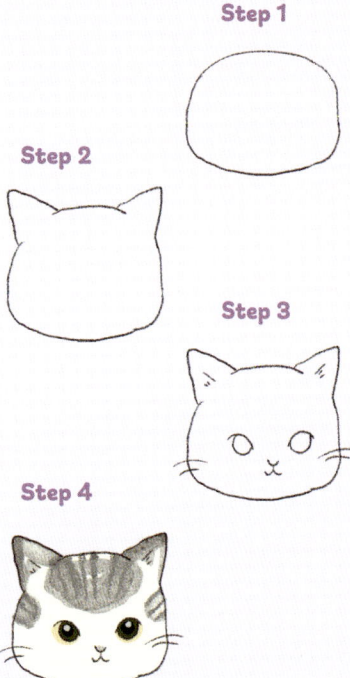

Step 1

Step 2

Step 3

Step 4

How to draw a cat's head in four steps

1 Using a pencil (not a ballpoint pen so that you can rub out the lines as in Step 2), begin by drawing a horizontal oval.

2 Next, draw 2 triangles on the upper part of the oval for ears. Rub out the lines between the oval and the 2 triangles.

3 Position the eyes just below the centre of the oval and add the muzzle by drawing a slightly splayed 'u' shape with a horizontal '3' below. Trace 2 whiskers on each side and then draw 3 small lines in each ear to create depth.

4 Finish the cat's head by adding colour, starting with the eyes. Leaving a small white circle, colour part of the eye black, then add dark grey around the black, finishing with a half-moon around the edge in a much lighter shade (cream, yellow or beige). Finish by colouring the whole head or by adding small touches of colour, depending on which you prefer (hopefully you will be inspired by the drawings below and opposite).

How to draw a cat's body

1 First draw the cat's head following steps 1–3 on the opposite page.

2 For the body, draw a second oval, positioned vertically and slightly smaller than the head, then add 2 short front legs downwards from the body. Rub out the dotted lines on the drawing.

3 Draw a smaller oval shape (like a rugby ball) to create the back of the body, then add the tail and a back leg. Rub out all the dotted lines to leave your final shape.

4 Finish the drawing by adding your chosen colours. For the head, follow step 4 described opposite.

Step 1

Step 2

Step 3

Step 4

Bento

Makes 4 bento
Prep time: 10 minutes
Marinating time:
30 minutes
Cooking time: 10 minutes

Ingredients

- **2 boneless chicken thighs**
- **1 garlic clove**
- **½ tablespoon grated fresh root ginger**
- **2 tablespoons soy sauce**
- **1 tablespoon sake**
- **potato flour**, spread out over a plate
- **oil**, for stir-frying
- **pepper**

Fried chicken kara-age

1 Cut the chicken into 8 pieces. Peel the garlic and crush the clove.

2 Mix the chicken cubes with the garlic, ginger, soy sauce, sake and a little pepper in a bowl. Cover and leave to marinate in the refrigerator for 30 minutes.

3 Drain the chicken cubes and toss them in the potato flour until evenly coated.

4 Heat a couple of tablespoons of oil in a wok and stir-fry the chicken, in 2 batches, for about 5 minutes until they are golden brown. Drain the chicken on kitchen paper.

TIP
For a vegetarian version, replace the chicken with firm tofu.

Step 1　　Step 2　　Step 3

Makes 4 bento
Prep time: 5 minutes
Cooking time: 5 minutes

Ingredients

- 6 eggs
- 100ml (3½fl oz) dashi stock (from Japanese food stores, optional)
- pinch of salt
- vegetable oil, for cooking

Omelette tamagoyaki

1 Beat the eggs, dashi stock and salt together in a bowl.

2 Heat a drizzle of oil in a tamagoyaki (rectangular) frying pan, then pour in a small amount of the beaten eggs and tilt the pan so the egg covers the base of it and sets to make a thin omelette.

3 Roll up the omelette from the back of the pan towards its handle.

4 Pour in another small amount of the beaten eggs. Gently lift the previously rolled omelette so a little of the egg flows under it. Cook until the egg mixture sets, then roll up this new omelette again from the back of the pan.

5 Repeat until you have used up all the beaten egg and made 4 thin rolled omelettes side by side in the pan. Cook the combined omelette until it is lightly golden on all sides, turning using a spatula. Turn it out on to a bamboo maki mat, fold the mat over the omelette and press with your hands to shape the omelette into neat rectangle.

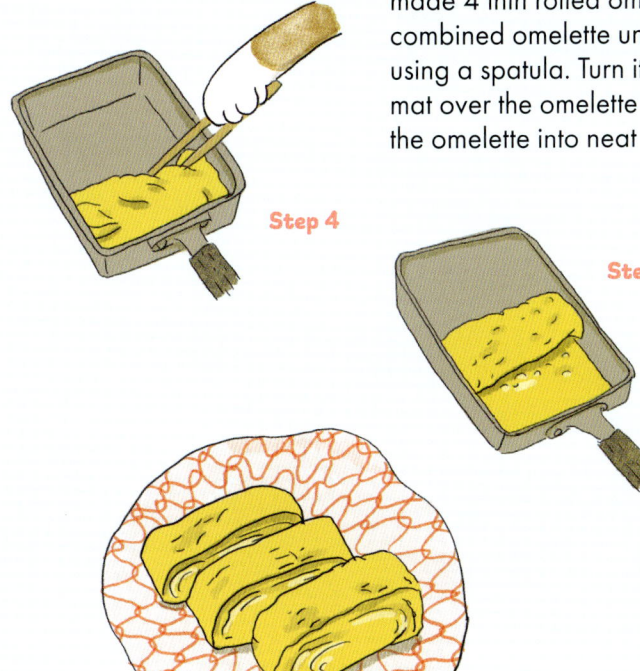

Step 4

Step 5

TIP

If you do not have a rectangular frying pan, a traditional round pan can be used to make an omelette with a slightly oval shape. Cut off both ends so it resembles the desired rectangle as closely as possible.

Makes 4 bento boxes
Prep time: 20 minutes
No cooking, apart from the broccoli, rice and chicken

Ingredients

- 1 Japanese omelette tamagoyaki (see recipe on previous page)
- 120g (4¼oz) steamed broccoli
- 4 small bowls of cooked rice (see page 26)
- 4 large lettuce leaves
- 8 pieces of kara-age chicken (see page 40)
- 8 cherry tomatoes

To decorate
- 1 sachet of inari (fried seasoned tofu, see page 50; this can be replaced with nori)
- 1 sheet of nori seaweed
- 1 slice of burger cheese

Assembling a bento box

1 Cut the omelette crosswise into slices about 1.5cm (⅝ inch) thick. Separate the broccoli into 4 florets.

2 Prepare the different items for decoration. Cut the inari tofu into 4 ovals for the cats' muzzles, 8 triangles for ears and 4 fish shapes. Cut eyes for the cats, whiskers, the black part of the muzzles and eyes for the fish from the nori seaweed. Cut out 8 tiny paw pads and 2 larger pads for each cat's paw from the cheese (you can make this easier by using different sized straws for cutting out).

3 Build your bento boxes; start by spooning the rice into the bottom half of each box.

4 Place a lettuce leaf in the remaining part of the boxes (this will form a barrier to keep the rice separate from the rest of the ingredients).

5 Next, add the kara-age chicken, the omelette slices and broccoli florets. Halve the cherry tomatoes and add.

6 Finish decorating the bento boxes by adding the different features to each cat's head. Position a fish under each muzzle and pads on the omelette tamagoyaki for paws.

The different types of sushi

As long as it always has vinegar-seasoned rice as a base, the shape of sushi can vary enormously.

- **Nigiri:** small ball of rice covered with a garnish.
- **Maki:** rolled sushi.
- **Temaki:** cone-shaped sushi, rolled by hand.
- **Temari:** ball-shaped sushi.
- **Gunkan:** sushi wrapped in a band of nori, topped with a garnish.
- **Oishi sushi:** square- or rectangular-shaped pressed sushi.

Cat sushi platter

Serves 4
Prep time: 5 minutes

Ingredients

Vinegared sushi rice
• 350g (12oz) hot cooked rice (see recipe, page 26)
• 2½ tablespoons rice vinegar for sushi

To garnish
• ¼ cucumber
• 4 shiso leaves (from Japanese food stores), or use mixed salad leaves
• 4 slices of very fresh (sushi grade) raw salmon
• 4 slices of very fresh (sushi grade) raw tuna
• 4 slices of tamagoyaki (see page 41)
• ½ sheet of nori seaweed

To serve
• soy sauce
• wasabi
• sushi pickled ginger

To prepare the vinegared sushi rice

1 Put the cooked rice, which should still be very hot, in a shallow dish and sprinkle with the rice vinegar for sushi.

2 Gently mix the rice using a rice spoon (or a flat spatula) to coat the grains but not crush them. While mixing, cool the rice with a fan to give it a beautifully shiny appearance.

Step 2

3 Let the rice rest covered with a damp tea towel to prevent it drying out while you prepare the garnishes.

To prepare the garnishes

4 Cut the cucumber into rectangular strips.

5 Place a cucumber strip and a shiso leaf on a sushi platter (or plate).

To shape the cats

6 Dampen your hands and place a small amount of vinegared rice in the palm of your hand. Lightly press the rice, rolling it into a small oval-shaped ball (for the cat's head). Shape 2 small triangles for ears.

7 Next, shape a small thinner ball for the cat's body and stick it to the head. Make 2 more cats with the vinegared rice in the same way.

8 Place the first cat on the cucumber strip on the sushi platter, a second one directly on the platter and a third on the shiso leaf.

9 Cover the first cat with a slice of salmon, the second with a slice of tuna and the third with a slice of tamagoyaki.

10 Dampen your hands again and take a small amount of rice to shape 2 legs. Position these either side of the neck of one of the cats.

11 Repeat with the other 3 platters.

To finish

12 Cut eyes, muzzles, whiskers and paw pads from the nori sheet (see page 16) and position them on the cats' faces for their features and the paw pads on the tamagoyaki.

Time to indulge!

Enjoy the cat sushi with soy sauce mixed with a dot of wasabi and pickled ginger.

TIP

You can, of course, make other styles of sushi, such as a strip of cucumber to cover the rice or a prawn that the cat can hold in its front paws. Use other types of fish or vegetables if you prefer.

See the next page for a photograph of this recipe.

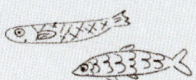

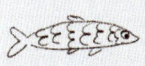

Inari zushi

Serves 4
(Makes 20 sushi)
Prep time: 50 minutes
Resting time: 20 minutes
Cooking time: 30 minutes

Ingredients

- 10 abura-age (fried tofu, available from Japanese food stores)
- 150ml (5fl oz) dashi stock (from Japanese food stores)
- 2 tablespoons soy sauce
- 2 tablespoons mirin
- 1 tablespoon sugar
- 4 small bowls of vinegared rice (see recipe, page 46)

To garnish and assemble
- 1 carrot
- ½ sheet of nori seaweed
- 20 dots of Dijon mustard
- **soy sauce, to serve**

To prepare the inari pockets

1 Place the pieces of fried tofu (abura-age) in a sieve and pour boiling water over them to remove a little of the fat. Drain and cut each piece in half.

2 Put the fried tofu pieces in a saucepan. Add the stock, soy sauce and mirin, followed by the sugar. Make sure that the fried tofu is completely covered with liquid. Bring to the boil and leave to cook over a low heat until there is no longer any liquid remaining. Set aside to cool.

To prepare the garnish

3 Peel the carrot and cut it into slices about 2mm (1/16 inch) thick. Cut the slices into 20 small flower shapes using a cutter. Blanch them in a saucepan of boiling water for 1 minute and then drain. Cut 20 pairs of eyes and whiskers from the nori sheet.

To shape and assemble the sushi

4 Dampen your hands to prevent the rice sticking to them. Lightly press the rice, rolling it into a small oval-shaped ball. Carefully open the fried tofu pockets and fill each one with a small ball of rice. Flatten the rice lightly to shape it into a cat's face. Decorate the face with nori eyes and whiskers and, using a cocktail stick, place a dot of mustard in the centre for the muzzle. Finally, place a carrot flower on the tofu hat.

5 Repeat using the remaining ingredients to make 20 sushi. Enjoy with a little soy sauce.

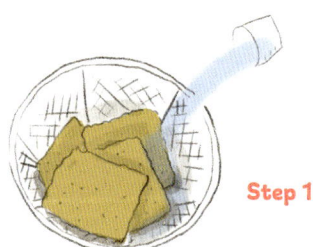

Step 1

Japanese kare rice

Serves 4
Prep time: 35 minutes
Cooking time: 30 minutes
(plus cooking the rice)

Ingredients

- 2 boneless chicken thighs
- 2 carrots
- ½ onion
- 8 button mushrooms
- sunflower oil, for frying
- 1 garlic clove, finely chopped
- 1 teaspoon finely chopped fresh root ginger
- 600ml (20fl oz) water
- 4 bowls of hot cooked rice (see page 26)
- 1 sheet of nori seaweed
- 80g (2¾oz) Japanese curry powder
- 2 hard-boiled eggs

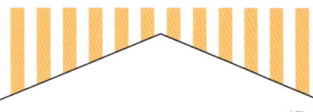

Step 6

1 Cut the chicken into bite-sized pieces.

2 Peel the carrots and chop them. Peel the onion and cut it into 8 wedges. Remove the woody part of the mushroom stalks and cut each into 4 pieces.

3 Heat a drizzle of sunflower oil in a flameproof casserole and fry the chopped garlic, ginger, carrots and onion wedges over a high heat for 3–4 minutes. Remove from the pan and set aside.

4 Add the chicken pieces, skin side down, to the same casserole and fry for 2 minutes until their skin is golden. Turn the pieces over and fry for a further 1 minute. Add the mushrooms and fry for 2–3 minutes. Return the vegetables to the casserole and pour in the measured water. Leave to cook for 15 minutes over a gentle heat.

5 Meanwhile, prepare 4 cat onigiri following steps 2, 3 and 4 on page 36. Also shape 8 front legs and 8 small balls of rice for paws. Decorate the paws with pads cut from the nori seaweed.

6 Mix the Japanese curry powder with a little of the cooking liquid in a ladle. Add to the casserole and leave to simmer for 5 minutes over a gentle heat, stirring constantly to incorporate the curry powder and thicken the sauce.

7 Divide the curry between soup plates, then position the different elements of the cats on top. Peel the hard-boiled eggs, cut in half and add them to the soup plates before serving.

Tonkatsu burgers

Serves 4
Prep time: 20 minutes
Cooking time: 10 minutes

Ingredients

For the tonkatsu pork
- 1 egg
- 4 tablespoons flour
- 4–6 tablespoons panko breadcrumbs
- 4 slices of pork loin, about 80g (2¾oz) each
- oil, for deep-frying
- salt and pepper

To serve
- 4 burger buns (see recipe opposite)
- 4 lettuce leaves
- ¼ green cabbage, grated
- tonkatsu sauce (from Japanese food stores, or a barbecue sauce)

1 First, prepare the tonkatsu pork. Beat the egg in a shallow dish. Spread out the flour on a plate and the breadcrumbs on another one. Season the pork with salt and pepper. Coat the slices of pork in the flour, dip them in the beaten egg and finally in the breadcrumbs, making sure that the crumb coating is sticking to them firmly.

2 Heat oil for deep-frying in a wok; it will have reached the correct temperature when bubbles appear around the edge of a small piece of bread dropped into it.

3 Deep-fry the pork slices, 2 at a time, in the hot oil for about 5 minutes until they are golden brown.

4 As soon as the pork slices are cooked, drain them from the wok on to a plate lined with kitchen paper.

5 To serve, split a burger bun in half and spread the base (the half without the ears) with tonkatsu sauce. Cover with a lettuce leaf and some grated cabbage. Add a slice of tonkatsu pork, coat again with tonkatsu sauce and cover with the burger bun lid.

6 Assemble the remaining burgers in the same way.

Step 1

Step 3

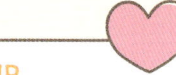

TIP
In Japan, tonkatsu is made with pork, but the recipe can be made equally well using chicken. Use boned chicken legs as the meat will be juicier and more tender than breast meat.

Makes 8 buns
Prep time: 30 minutes
Rising time: 1 hour
45 minutes
Cooking time: 12 minutes

Ingredients

- 1 tablespoon dried yeast
- 2½ tablespoons caster sugar
- 120ml (4fl oz) hot water (about 70°C/158°F)
- 300g (10½oz) plain white flour
- 1 teaspoon salt
- 1 egg, beaten
- 35g (1¼oz) butter, at room temperature

To finish
- 1 egg
- pinch of salt
- 1 tablespoon water
- 1 fine black food-safe decorating pen

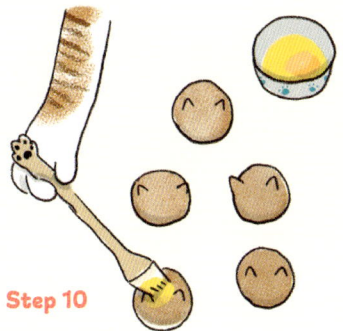

Step 10

Recipe for making burger buns

1 Dissolve the yeast and sugar in the hot water in a bowl and set aside for 5 minutes.

2 Sift the flour and salt into a mixing bowl. Add the yeast mixture and mix well.

3 Add the beaten egg and mix again.

4 Cut the butter into cubes, gradually incorporate it into the dough and then knead for 10 minutes. The dough must be stretchy but not stick to your fingers. If necessary, add a little extra water if the dough is too dry, or flour if the dough is too sticky.

5 Shape the dough into a ball and place it in a clean mixing bowl. Cover with a tea towel and leave to rest in a warm place for 1 hour or until the dough has doubled in volume.

6 When the dough has doubled in size, knead it briskly to burst any air bubbles inside. Set aside 1 ball of dough the size of a ping-pong ball which will be used to make the ears.

7 Shape the remaining dough into a ball once again and cut it into 8 equal-sized pieces. Roll each piece into a small ball and place the balls, well-spaced apart, on a baking sheet lined with baking parchment. Lightly press the top of each bun to flatten it slightly.

8 Shape small triangles from the reserved ball of dough and stick 2 on each of the 8 balls for the cats' ears. Cover loosely with clingfilm and leave to prove for 45 minutes.

9 Preheat the oven to 200°C (400°F), Gas Mark 6.

10 Beat the egg in a bowl with the pinch of salt and the water and brush over the balls of dough to glaze them.

11 Bake for 12 minutes or until the tops of the buns are golden brown. Transfer to a wire rack and leave to cool for 10 minutes. Using the decorating pen, draw cats' features on the top of each bun (see page 16).

Ja-purr-nese ravioli

Gyoza are totally addictive! These Japanese-style ravioli have a unique texture – they are toasted and crisp on one side but steamed on the other side, which remains soft.

Let me offer you two important pieces of advice:

1 Invite your friends over for a group cook-in, it will save you time!

2 Use a good non-stick frying pan for cooking.

Gyoza

Makes 24 gyoza
Prep time: 30 minutes
Cooking time: 10–15 minutes

Ingredients

• 24 gyoza wrappers (see page 62, or from Japanese food stores)

For the stuffing
• 120g (4¼oz) green cabbage
• 120g (4¼oz) minced pork
• 1 spring onion, finely chopped
• 1 garlic clove, finely chopped
• 1 teaspoon grated fresh root ginger
• 3 tablespoons soy sauce
• 3 teaspoons toasted sesame oil, plus extra for cooking
• salt and pepper

For the dipping sauce and to decorate
• 2 tablespoons rice vinegar
• 2 tablespoons soy sauce
• ½ sheet of nori seaweed or 1 fine black food-safe decorating pen

To make the stuffing

1 Blanch the cabbage leaves for 1 minute in a saucepan of boiling water. Drain and chop the leaves finely. Place in a bowl and mix in all the other stuffing ingredients.

To shape the gyoza

2 Place a generous teaspoonful of the stuffing in the centre of each gyoza wrapper. Dampen the edge of the upper part of the wrappers and fold them in half over the stuffing, making sure as little air as possible is trapped inside. Press the edges together with your thumb so the gyoza are tightly sealed.

Step 2

3 Using scissors, trim the edges of the wrappers to shape the ears.

To cook the gyoza

4 Heat a drizzle of oil in a frying pan, arrange the gyoza in the pan in a rosette/circle and cook for 3 minutes on each side until they are golden.

5 Pour in water to come halfway up the sides, cover and leave to cook over a gentle heat until the water has completely evaporated. Remove the lid, pour in a small drizzle of oil and cook for a further 1 minute.

Finish and enjoy!

6 Make the sauce by mixing the rice vinegar and soy sauce together.

7 Place the gyoza on a serving plate and decorate them with cat faces, cutting the features from the sheet of nori seaweed (see the technique page 16) or using a food-safe decorating pen.

8 To eat, dip the gyoza into the sauce.

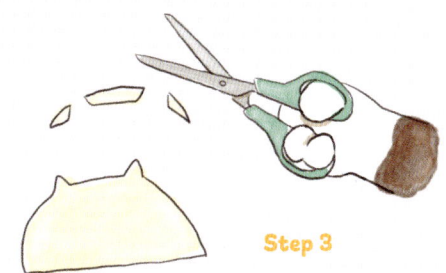

Step 3

Step 5

TIP
The stuffing can be varied by replacing the minced pork with chicken breast or prawns, for example.

Makes 24 gyoza wrappers

Ingredients

- **75g (2½oz) plain white flour**
- **75g (2½oz) rice flour**
- **100ml (3½fl oz) water**

Recipe for making gyoza dough

You can also make this dough yourself!

1 Mix both flours together in a bowl. Add the water and mix with your hand until you have a smooth dough. Cover with a damp tea towel and set aside for 15 minutes.

2 Roll the dough into a sausage shape and cut into 24 equal pieces. Gently flatten 1 piece of dough and place it between 2 sheets of clingfilm. Roll out, pressing down on the dough with a flat plate to help you cut out a disc, about 10cm (4 inches) in diameter. Repeat with the remaining pieces of dough.

 TIP
Although gyoza dough freezes very well, remember to flour between each layer generously before stacking and freezing the rounds of dough to make it easier to separate them once thawed.

Soboro bento boxes

Serves 4
Prep time: 35 minutes
Cooking time: 12 minutes

Ingredients

For the soboro meat
- 400g (14oz) minced pork (or minced beef)
- ½ tablespoon cornflour
- sunflower oil, for frying
- 1 spring onion, chopped
- 1 tablespoon grated fresh root ginger
- 2 tablespoons soy sauce
- 2 tablespoons caster sugar
- 3 tablespoons miso paste
- 1 tablespoon toasted sesame oil

For the scrambled eggs
- 4 eggs
- salt and pepper

To assemble and decorate
- 4 small bowls of hot cooked rice (see page 26)
- 1 strip of nori seaweed
- ½ slice of cooked ham
- 1 slice of burger cheese
- 12 small carrot flowers (see page 50)

To prepare the soboro meat

1 Mix the minced pork with the cornflour in a large bowl.

2 Heat a drizzle of sunflower oil in a wok and stir-fry the meat with the spring onion and ginger over a high heat for 4–5 minutes. Season with the soy sauce and sugar. Toss everything together and cook for 3 minutes. Remove the pan from the heat and mix in the miso and sesame oil.

To prepare the scrambled eggs

3 Beat the eggs in a bowl with a pinch of salt and a grind of pepper. Heat a drizzle of oil in a non-stick frying pan, then pour in the eggs. When they begin to set, mix with chopsticks or a spatula until the consistency of scrambled eggs.

To assemble the bento boxes

4 Cover the base of a bento box with a thin layer of rice, then spread one-quarter of the soboro meat over one-third of the surface. Next, spoon half a bowl of rice in the centre of the bento, covering another third of it, and finish with one-quarter of the scrambled eggs in the remaining third. Gently press down on the surface of the 3 ingredients to even them out a little. Repeat, spooning the remaining ingredients into 3 more bento boxes.

To decorate the bento boxes

5 Cut the cats' features (eyes, whiskers, muzzle and ears) from the nori seaweed, the ham and the cheese. Arrange in each bento box to create 3 different-coloured cats' faces, as shown in the photograph opposite. Complete by decorating with the carrot flowers.

Sando

Serves 4
Prep time: 20 minutes
Resting time: 5 minutes
Cooking time: 8 minutes

Ingredients

- 6 eggs
- 4 tablespoons Japanese Kewpie mayonnaise
- 8 slices of sandwich bread
- salt and pepper

To garnish
- 1 strip of nori seaweed
- dash of ketchup
- 2 parsley sprigs
- 1 handful of mixed salad leaves (optional)
- several cherry tomatoes (optional)

To hard-boil the eggs

1 Bring a saucepan of water to the boil. Carefully lower the eggs into the water and cook for 8 minutes. Drain and immediately plunge the eggs in cold water to prevent them from cooking any more. Peel off the shells.

To prepare the sandwiches

2 Chop the eggs into small dice, place in a bowl and carefully mix with the mayonnaise. Season with salt and pepper.

3 Spread the egg mixture over 4 slices of the bread and top with the remaining slices. Set aside between 2 chopping boards so the sandwiches retain their shape.

To finish the sando

4 Meanwhile, prepare the cats' features, cuttings eyes, muzzles and whiskers from the nori seaweed.

5 Using a large cutter in the shape of a cat's face, cut out 4 tamago sando (Japanese egg sandwich). Create the faces by positioning the eyes, muzzles and whiskers cut from the nori seaweed. Add dots of ketchup for the cheeks and decorate each face with a parsley leaf.

6 If you wish, accompany the sandwiches with a mixed leaf and cherry tomato salad.

Step 5

Kitsuné udon

Serves 4
Prep time: 25 minutes
Cooking time: 10 minutes

Ingredients
• 250g (9oz) dried udon noodles

For the stock
• 1.2 litres (2 pints) dashi stock
• 3 tablespoons soy sauce
• 2 tablespoons mirin
• ½ tablespoon sugar

To garnish
• 1 sheet of nori seaweed
• 4 inari (fried tofu pockets, see recipe page 50, step 1)
• 8 slices of naruto (spiral-shaped Japanese surimi, optional)
• 1 small spring onion, green part cut into small strips and kept in a bowl of cold water to make them curl
• 4 carrot flowers (see page 50)

To make the stock

1 Bring all the stock ingredients to the boil in a saucepan and boil for 3 minutes. Set aside but keep hot.

To prepare the garnishes and cook the noodles

2 Make the decorations for the cats' faces by cutting the eyes, muzzles and whiskers from the sheet of nori seaweed (see page 16). Using a cutter, cut the inari pockets into cat shapes.

3 Cook the udon noodles in a saucepan of boiling water according to the packet instructions (4–5 minutes) and then drain them.

4 Divide the noodles between 4 large bowls. Pour the hot stock over them, then place an inari cat face on top. Arrange the features cut from the nori seaweed on the cats' faces.

5 Garnish with the naruto slices (if using), spring onion strips and place a carrot flower in each bowl.

6 Serve piping hot!

Step 2

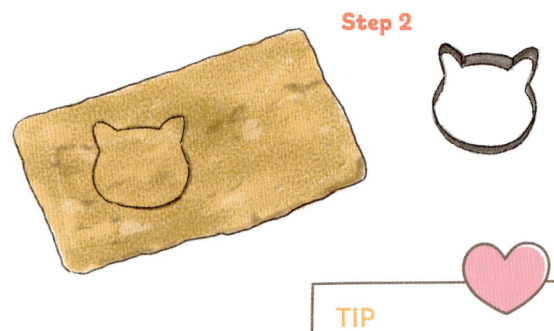

TIP
Naruto can be found in the frozen section of Japanese food stores. It can be replaced with surimi or a strip of nori seaweed.

Japanese street food

Japanese cuisine is about so much more than sushi and, as is the case in the rest of Asia, Japan has a street food culture where it is normal to eat while on the move. Street food is everywhere and very varied. Discover two recipes that are particularly popular in the pages that follow: manju and korokke.

Manju dumplings

Makes 8 manju
Prep time: 40 minutes
Soaking and rising time: 50 minutes
Cooking time: 15 minutes

Ingredients

- 1 dried shiitake mushroom

For the dough
- 275g (9¾oz) plain white flour, 5g (⅛oz) for kneading and extra for dusting
- 20g (¾oz) sugar
- 1 teaspoon active dry yeast
- 1 teaspoon baking powder
- ½ teaspoon salt
- 1 tablespoon vegetable oil
- 150ml (5fl oz) warm water

For the stuffing
- 250g (9oz) minced pork
- ½ onion, finely chopped
- 1 teaspoon grated fresh root ginger
- ½ tablespoon soy sauce
- ½ tablespoon miso
- ½ tablespoon toasted sesame oil
- ½ tablespoon potato flour (or cornflour)
- pinch of pepper

To decorate
- 1 fine black food-safe decorating pen
- finely sliced green top of 1 spring onion, for sprinkling

1 Begin by soaking the shiitake mushroom in a small bowl of water for 20 minutes.

To make the dough

2 Mix the flour, sugar, yeast, baking powder and salt together in a large bowl.

3 Stir in the oil, then gradually mix in the warm water until you have a soft, supple dough.

4 Dust the worktop with the extra 5g (⅛oz) flour and knead the dough for about 10 minutes.

5 Shape the dough into a ball, place it in a clean mixing bowl and cover with a damp tea towel. Leave in a warm, draught-free place for at least 30 minutes until it has doubled in volume.

To make the stuffing

6 Drain the soaked shiitake mushroom, squeezing it thoroughly with your hands to remove excess water. Remove the stalk and chop finely. Mix all the stuffing ingredients together in a bowl.

To shape the dumplings

7 Remove the dough from the mixing bowl to a worktop dusted with flour and shape it into a cylinder.

8 Cut the cylinder into 8 equal pieces, then roll each into a round, about 10cm (4 inches) in diameter.

9 Place a large tablespoonful (or use an ice-cream scoop) of the stuffing in the centre of each dough round.

10 Holding a round of dough in one hand and keeping your thumb on the stuffing, use the thumb and index finger of the other hand to pinch the dough together at regular intervals to enclose the stuffing. Working around the dough, pinch the edges until the dumpling is well sealed at the top.

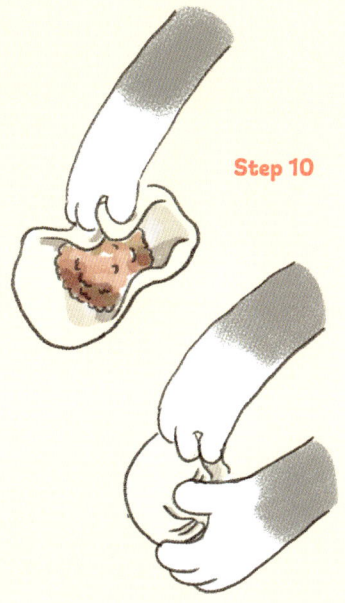

Step 10

11 Trim off the excess dough and use it to shape 2 small cats' ears on the top of the brioche/dumpling.

12 Proceed in the same way for the rest of the manju, then place the dumplings on a square of baking parchment in a steamer basket (leaving sufficient space between them as they will puff up).

13 Heat water in the saucepan over which you are going to place the steamer basket, without bringing the water to the boil. Turn off the heat under the pan, place the basket on top of the steamer and leave the dumplings to rise for 20 minutes.

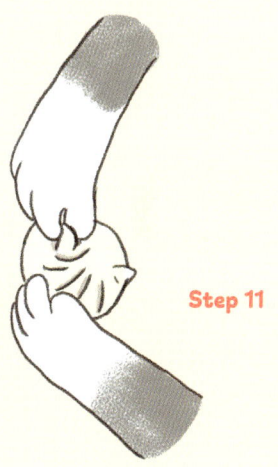

Step 11

14 Steam the manju for 15 minutes.

15 Add the cats' features using a food-safe marker pen following the instructions on page 16 and sprinkle a little finely sliced spring onion on top of each.

16 Eat the manju with the sauce of your choice (such as soy, sweet and sour sauce, or chilli sauce).

Origami

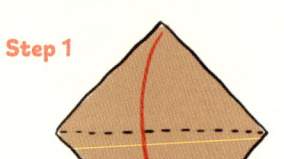
Step 1

Try your hand at making an origami cat. It will prove extra useful as a cute bookmark.

1 Fold a sheet of origami paper diagonally (the coloured part on the inside).

2 Fold again as shown.

3 Fold once more, then unfold.

4 Lift the first layer in the centre.

5 Bend the left point towards the right point.

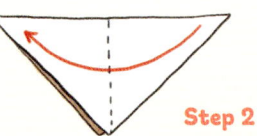
Step 2

6 Turn the origami paper over and do the same again. You will now have a square.

7 Lift the point of the top sheet and fold it down towards point A.

8 Turn the origami over and do the same again.

9 Rotate the fold 90 degrees clockwise and fold the bottom point down on to the centre point.

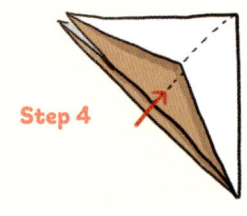
Step 3

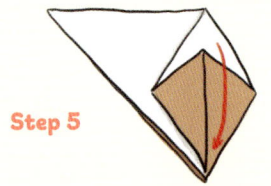
Step 4

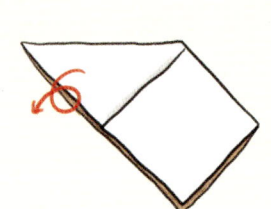
Step 5

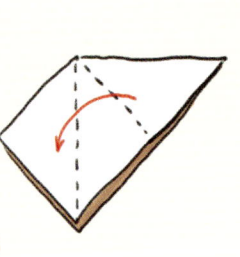
Step 6

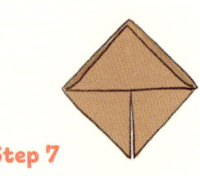
Step 7

Step 8

Step 9

Step 10

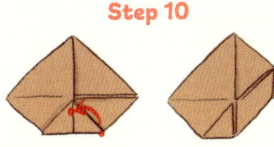

Step 11

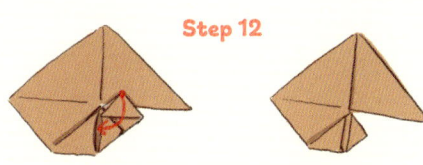

Step 12

10 Then fold the left point as shown.

11 Bend the left point towards the central point.

12 Then fold the tab and insert it into the slit.

Step 13

9, 10, 11, 12

Step 14

13 Do the same again (steps 9, 10, 11 and 12) on the opposite side.

14 Fold down the remaining point opposite the ears following the dotted lines.

15 Unfold the point you have just folded, pull the first point towards you and fold the remaining 2 points into the slit.

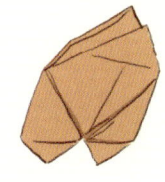

Step 15

16 Insert the remaining point into the same slit.

17 Turn the fold over and your cat's head is ready to be decorated!

Step 16

Step 17

Korokke, crunchy croquettes!

Makes 12–16 korokke (depending on size)
Prep time: 30 minutes
Cooking time: 10 minutes

Ingredients
- 6 medium potatoes, unpeeled
- sunflower oil, for frying
- 1 onion, finely chopped
- 1 carrot, peeled and finely chopped
- 200g (7oz) minced beef
- 2 eggs
- 2 tablespoons potato flour
- 50g (1¾oz) panko breadcrumbs
- tonkatsu sauce (available from Japanese food stores but can be replaced with ketchup)
- salt and pepper

To decorate
- 1 fine black food-safe decorating pen

To prepare the croquette mixture

1 Cook the potatoes in a saucepan of boiling salted water for about 20 minutes. Drain the potatoes and peel off their skins. Transfer to a bowl and mash with a fork.

2 Heat a drizzle of sunflower oil in a frying pan and fry the onion and carrot over a medium heat for 3 minutes. Add the minced beef and season with salt. Increase the heat to high and fry for another 4–5 minutes, stirring occasionally to break up any lumps of meat.

3 Add to the mashed potatoes in the bowl and mix well.

4 Separate the eggs.

5 Add the egg yolks to the beef mixture, mixing them in thoroughly. Season again with salt and also pepper.

To shape the croquettes

6 Using your hands, shape the beef mixture into 12–16 small balls (depending on the size you wish to make them). Mould 2 ears on each ball.

To coat the croquettes

7 Beat the eggs whites in a bowl until frothy. Spread the potato flour over a plate and the breadcrumbs over another plate. Carefully coat the croquettes in the flour, then with the egg whites and finally with the breadcrumbs.

Step 1

Step 2

To cook the croquettes

8 Heat sunflower oil for deep-frying in a wok and deep-fry the croquettes (in batches) for about 5 minutes until they are golden brown. Drain the croquettes on kitchen paper.

To finish and enjoy!

9 Draw on the cats' faces with the food-safe decorating pen.

10 Serve accompanied with the tonkatsu sauce.

Step 3

Step 6

Step 7

TIP
Double fried
For maximum crunchiness, it is worth frying the croquettes twice. For the first fry, heat the oil to 160°C (325°F) and fry the croquettes until they are lightly golden. Remove them from the wok and drain well for 5 minutes. Increase the temperature of the oil to 180°C (350°F) and fry the croquettes a second time until they are golden brown.

See the next page for a photograph of this recipe.

Japanese patisserie

While traditional sweet dishes such as wagashi are often eaten at teatime, western desserts with a Japanese twist (such as matcha tiramisu) are becoming increasingly popular. However, many recipes are still prepared with anko (or an), a paste made from azuki beans, which is used as the base for many Japanese pastries. See the recipe on page 84.

Anko: azuki red bean paste

Makes 1kg (2lb 4oz) anko paste
Soaking time: 12 hours
Prep time: 20 minutes
Cooking time: 2 hours 10 minutes

Ingredients
- 500g (1lb 2oz) dried red azuki beans (available from health food shops or Asian food stores)
- 360g (12½oz) caster sugar

1 Soak the beans in a large quantity of cold water for at least 12 hours.

2 Drain, rinse and place the beans in a saucepan. Cover them with cold water, bring to the boil and then drain.

3 Return the beans to the saucepan and cover with at least twice their volume of water. Bring to the boil and cook for 1½–2 hours, making sure to top up the water when necessary.

4 The beans are cooked when they can be crushed easily between your fingers. Drain the beans.

5 Mix the beans and sugar together in a heavy-based saucepan and, stirring constantly, cook for a further 10 minutes.

Step 1

Step 2

Step 3

Step 4

Step 5

TIP
To obtain a smooth paste, push the beans in batches through a sturdy sieve (or vegetable mill) between steps 4 and 5 on the opposite page.

Anpan meow

Makes 10
Prep time: 30 minutes
Cooking time: 12 minutes
Rising and resting time:
1 hour 45 minutes

Ingredients

- 50g (1¾oz) caster sugar
- 1½ teaspoons dried yeast
- 100ml (3½fl oz) milk
- 250g (9oz) plain white flour, plus extra for dusting
- 1 tablespoon cornflour
- 1 teaspoon salt
- 1 egg, beaten
- 35g (1¼oz) butter, at room temperature
- 320g (11½oz) anko (azuki red bean paste, see page 84)

To finish
- 1 egg
- 1 tablespoon water
- pinch of salt
- melted plain dark chocolate, for adding the cats' faces

1 Stir the sugar and yeast into the milk in a bowl and set aside for 5 minutes.

2 Sift the flour, cornflour and salt into a mixing bowl. Add the milk mixture and stir in.

3 Add the beaten egg and mix again. Dice the butter and work it into the dough. Knead for 10 minutes (or for 4 minutes using a hand-held electric whisk). The dough must be smooth and stretchy but not stick to your fingers. Adjust the consistency if necessary, adding more milk if the dough is too dry or more flour if it is too sticky.

4 Shape the dough into a ball and place it in a clean mixing bowl. Cover with a tea towel and leave the dough to rise in a warm place for 1 hour until it has doubled in volume.

5 When the dough has doubled in volume, knead it briefly to burst any air bubbles inside. Shape into a ball again and cut it into 10 equal pieces.

6 Roll each piece to form small balls. Line a baking sheet with baking parchment and place the dough balls on it. Cover with clingfilm and leave to rest for 15 minutes.

Step 5

7 Meanwhile, shape the anko paste into 10 balls using an ice-cream scoop.

8 Dust your work surface with flour. Take a ball of dough, roll it into a round about 10cm (4 inches) in diameter and place a ball of anko paste in the centre. Wrap the dough around the paste to enclose it completely. Cut off the excess dough and shape into 2 triangles. Stick these on top to make the cat's ears. Repeat with the remaining dough and paste.

9 Leave to rest for 30 minutes on a baking sheet covered with clingfilm. Preheat the oven to 200°C (400°F), Gas Mark 6.

10 To finish, beat the egg in a bowl with the water and pinch of salt and brush over the dough balls to glaze them.

11 Bake in the oven for 12 minutes. Leave to cool until lukewarm and then draw on the cats' faces and paws with melted chocolate using a toothpick.

Step 8

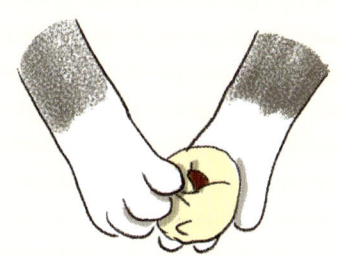

See the next page for a photograph of this recipe.

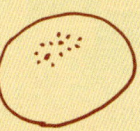

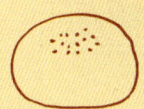

Mango mochi

Makes 6
Prep time: 25 minutes
Cooking time: 15 minutes
Freezing time: at least 3 hours

Ingredients

For the filling
- 50g (1¾oz) mascarpone cheese
- 120ml (4fl oz) whipping cream, well-chilled
- 70g (2½oz) icing sugar
- 90g (3¼oz) fresh mango flesh

For the dough
- 100g (3½oz) glutinous rice flour
- 50g (1¾oz) icing sugar
- 150ml (5fl oz) water
- potato flour, for dusting

To decorate
- melted plain dark chocolate

To make the filling

1 Whip the mascarpone, cream and icing sugar together in a bowl until stiff.

2 Meanwhile, cut the mango flesh into small dice.

3 Line a small bowl with clingfilm and spread it with some of the whipped cream mixture. Add a spoonful of the diced mango and cover this with more cream. Wrap the clingfilm around the mixture to shape it into a ball. Repeat using the rest of the mango and the cream mixture to make 6 balls. Place them in the freezer for at least 3 hours (ideally overnight).

To make the dough

4 Whisk the glutinous rice flour, icing sugar and water together in a bowl until smooth.

5 Heat water in the bottom of a steamer. Place the bowl in the steamer basket, cover and cook for 15 minutes. Check to ensure the mixture is cooked in the centre and, if there is any liquid remaining, continue cooking for a few more minutes.

6 Sift potato flour on to a work surface and tip the cooked dough on to it. Coat the dough with the flour as it will be very sticky (do not be afraid to use a lot). Roll out the dough until it is about 1cm (½ inch) thick and cut it into 6 pieces.

7 Take the cream and mango balls out of the freezer. Remove the clingfilm and place 1 on a piece of rolled-out dough. Carefully wrap the dough around the ball and seal the join. Cut off a small piece of dough at the seal, shape 2 ears from it and stick these on the top. Repeat with the remaining 5 balls and dough.

8 Decorate the head of each cat with melted chocolate (see the technique on page 17).

Step 3

Cat tongue cookies

Makes about 20 cookies
Prep time: 30 minutes
Cooking time: 5 minutes
Resting time: 45 minutes

Ingredients
- 60g (2¼oz) plain white flour
- pinch of salt
- 45g (1½oz) butter, at room temperature
- 45g (1½oz) icing sugar
- 1 sachet or 1½ teaspoons of vanilla sugar
- 1 egg

To decorate
- 150g (5½oz) white chocolate
- 1 drop of pink food colouring

Equipment
- silicone langue de chat mould
- piping bag

1 Preheat the oven to 180°C (350°F), Gas Mark 4.

2 Sift the flour and salt into a bowl. Set aside.

3 In another bowl, vigorously whisk (preferably using a hand-held electric whisk) the butter, icing sugar and vanilla sugar together. Add the egg and then whisk again until the mixture is evenly combined.

4 Next, fold in the flour and salt.

5 Spoon the mixture into a piping bag and pipe the mixture into the cavities in the langue de chat mould.

6 Bake for about 5 minutes or until the edges of the biscuits are golden.

7 Leave the biscuits to cool.

8 Meanwhile, melt 100g (3½oz) white chocolate squares in a bain-marie (a heatproof bowl over a pan of simmering water).

9 When the biscuits are cold, dip one end of each biscuit (about 2cm/¾ inch) in the melted chocolate. Leave until the chocolate has set.

10 Melt the remaining chocolate in the bain-marie again, adding a drop of food colouring to tint it a pretty pink. Using a small paper piping cone, pipe the pink chocolate on the end of each biscuit dipped in white chocolate to create paw pads.

Step 9

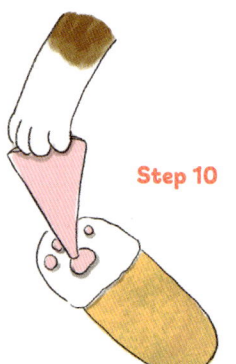
Step 10

TIP

If possible, bake these biscuits in a mould to give them a good shape. They can also be baked without using a mould by piping on to a lined baking sheet, but it is important to ensure the biscuits do not become too wide as the dough tends to spread during baking.

Matcha tirami-cats

Serves 8
Prep time: 20 minutes
No cooking required
Chilling time: at least
3 hours

Ingredients

- 2 fresh organic eggs
- 60g (2¼oz) caster sugar
- 200g (7oz) mascarpone cheese
- pinch of salt
- ½ tablespoon matcha green tea powder
- 120ml (4fl oz) hot water
- 16 sponge fingers (boudoir biscuits)

To decorate
- 1 tablespoon matcha green tea powder
- melted plain dark chocolate

To make the mascarpone cream

1 Separate the egg whites and yolks. Beat the egg yolks in a mixing bowl with the sugar and then add the mascarpone, beating until the mixture is smooth.

2 Whisk the egg whites with the salt until standing in firm peaks, then gently fold them into the mascarpone mixture.

To assemble the dessert

3 Infuse the ½ tablespoon matcha green tea powder in a bowl containing the hot water.

4 Dip the sponge fingers one at a time into the tea, then place a layer of them side by side in the base of 8 small square dishes (or ramekins), trimming them to fit neatly, if necessary.

5 Spoon a little of the mascarpone cream over the sponge fingers. Add another layer of sponge fingers and finish with another layer of mascarpone cream.

6 Smooth the surface of each with a spatula and place the dishes in the refrigerator to chill for at least 3 hours, preferably overnight.

To decorate the tirami-cats

7 Remove the dishes from the refrigerator. Place a stencil in the shape of a cat's head on 1 of the dishes and, using a fine sieve, dust the top of the dessert around the stencil with the matcha green tea powder.

8 Remove the stencil and decorate the cat's face with melted chocolate.

9 Decorate the remaining tirami-cats in the same way.

Step 7

Ice cream in Japan

During their country's hot, humid summers, the Japanese keep cool by eating ice cream in various forms: in cornets (cones) with flavours that are unique to Japan (such as matcha, sesame and yuzu), in mochi, as soft ice cream, or as shaved ice (kakigori), which has a light, airy texture similar to snow.

Neko ice cream

Makes 1.2 litres (2 pints)
Prep time: 15 minutes
Cooking time: 5 minutes
Cooling and chilling time: 30 minutes
Churning time: 25 minutes

Ingredients
- 120g (4¼oz) caster sugar
- 6 egg yolks
- 750ml (1 ⅓ pints) milk
- 250ml (9fl oz) crème fraîche
- 1 vanilla pod

To decorate
- ice-cream cones
- strawberries
- whole unblanched almonds
- melted plain dark chocolate

TIP
Be careful not to overcook the mixture, as it could set. To avoid this you could use a bain-marie, which allows for more gentle cooking.

1 Whisk the sugar and egg yolks on high speed in a mixing bowl until thick and mousse-like.

2 Pour the milk and crème fraîche into a saucepan. Split the vanilla pod lengthwise, scrape out the seeds with the back of a teaspoon and add to the milk and crème fraîche in the saucepan. Heat gently over a low heat, bring to the boil and then remove the saucepan from the heat.

3 Pour the still hot mixture on to the sugar and egg yolks, whisking constantly until evenly combined and very smooth.

4 Return the mixture to the saucepan. Using a wooden spoon, stir constantly over a low heat until the custard thickens.

5 As soon as the mixture coats the back of the spoon, and when you draw your finger through it the line does not close up again, take the saucepan off the heat.

6 Press a sheet of clingfilm over the surface of the custard and leave to cool for 15 minutes at room temperature before transferring to the refrigerator.

7 When the custard is completely cold, remove the clingfilm and the vanilla pod and pour it into an ice-cream maker. Churn for about 25 minutes.

8 Using an ice-cream scoop, put 2 scoops in a cone. Place a strawberry on top and an almond either side of it. Use melted chocolate to add the cat's features, following the instructions on page 17.

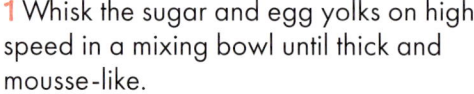

Step 8

Doughnuts

Makes 8
Prep time: 35 minutes
Rising and resting time: 2½ hours
Cooking time: 12 minutes

Ingredients

For the dough
- 1½ teaspoons dried yeast
- 120ml (4fl oz) warm milk
- 50g (1¾oz) caster sugar
- 1 tablespoon vanilla sugar
- 1 teaspoon baking powder
- 1 egg
- pinch of salt
- 300g (10½oz) plain white flour, plus extra for dusting
- 30g (1oz) butter, diced, at room temperature
- oil, for deep-frying

To decorate
- 200g (7oz) icing sugar
- 1 egg white
- juice of ¼ lemon
- melted plain dark chocolate

To make the dough

1 Dissolve the yeast in the milk in a bowl. Pour into a mixing bowl and add the sugar, vanilla sugar, baking powder, egg and salt. Whisk all the ingredients together until smooth.

2 Add the flour and mix it in, followed by the diced butter. Knead by hand for 10 minutes (or for 4 minutes in a stand mixer fitted with the dough hook attachment). The dough must be supple but not sticking to your fingers. Adjust the consistency if necessary, adding a little milk if it is too dry, or flour if the dough is too sticky.

Leaving the dough to rise

3 Shape the dough into a ball and place it in a clean mixing bowl. Cover with a damp tea towel and leave the dough to rise in a warm place for 1 hour or until it has doubled in volume.

4 When the dough has doubled in volume, cut it into 8 equal-sized pieces.

5 Quickly knead each piece again to burst any air bubbles inside and shape into small balls. Line a baking sheet with baking parchment and place the balls of dough on it. Cover with a tea towel and leave to prove for 15 minutes.

Shaping the doughnuts

6 Dust the work surface with flour. Take a ball of dough and roll it to a round, about 8cm (3¼ inches) in diameter. Shape the cat's ears by lightly pinching the dough between your thumb and forefinger.

7 Using a cutter about 3cm (1 ¼ inches) in diameter (or a small glass), cut a hole in the centre and remove the piece of dough. Place the doughnut on a square of baking parchment.

Step 7

8 Repeat with the remaining 7 doughnuts.

9 Leave the 8 doughnuts to rest for 1 hour, covered with a tea towel.

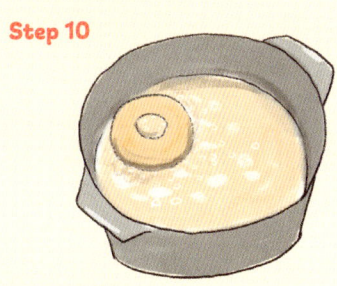
Step 10

Frying the doughnuts

10 In a deep pan, heat the oil to 180°C (350°F) for deep-frying and lower the doughnuts (cook them in batches) into the oil. Fry over a low heat so the doughnuts are an even golden colour underneath (2 minutes maximum). Turn them over and cook for about another 1 ½ minutes. Drain the doughnuts on to kitchen paper.

11 Fry all the doughnuts in the same way and leave them to cool until they are lukewarm.

Decorating the doughnuts

12 While the doughnuts are frying, make the icing. Whisk together the icing sugar, egg white and lemon juice in a shallow dish that is larger than the diameter of the doughnuts.

Step 13

13 Dip the tops of the doughnuts in the icing and place them on a wire rack, icing uppermost. Leave for 15 minutes until the icing has set. Dip the doughnuts a second time if you would like the icing to be more opaque.

14 Once the icing has set, add the cats' features using melted chocolate, following the instructions on page 17.

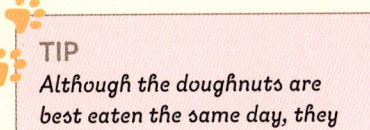

TIP
Although the doughnuts are best eaten the same day, they can be kept for 2–3 days in an airtight container.

See the next page for a photograph of this recipe.

Meow meow biscuits

Makes about 30 biscuits
Prep time: 25 minutes
Chilling time: 50 minutes
Cooking time: 10 minutes

Ingredients

- 150g (5½oz) plain white flour
- 80g (2¾oz) caster sugar
- 40g (1½oz) ground almonds
- pinch of salt
- 70g (2½oz) butter, diced, at room temperature
- 1 egg
- 1 teaspoon unsweetened cocoa powder

To decorate
- melted plain dark chocolate

1 Mix the flour, sugar, ground almonds and salt together in the bowl of a food processor. Add the diced butter and process on medium speed until the mixture resembles fine crumbs. Next, add the egg and process again to make a soft dough that is not too sticky or too dry, adjusting the texture, if necessary, by adding a little extra flour or water.

2 Weigh out about 50g (1¾oz) of the dough and work the cocoa powder into this until it is evenly dark brown in colour. Shape into a ball and cover with clingfilm.

3 Cover the rest of the dough with clingfilm and chill both pieces in the refrigerator for at least 30 minutes.

4 Unwrap the ball of plain dough and roll it out between 2 sheets of baking parchment until it is 1cm (½ inch) thick. Divide the chocolate dough into about 20 pieces and roll into tiny balls. Place them on the dough that has already been rolled out, evenly spaced apart. Lightly press down on each ball with your thumb, cover with a sheet of baking parchment and, roll into an even layer about 6mm (¼ inch) thick. Chill again for 20 minutes.

5 Preheat the oven to 180°C (350°F), Gas Mark 4.

6 Using a pastry cutter in the shape of a cat's head, cut out about 30 biscuits from the rolled out dough, cutting the shapes as closely together as possible.

7 Line a large baking sheet with baking parchment and lift the cut-out biscuits on to it. Bake for about 10 minutes or until the edges of the biscuits are lightly golden.

8 Cool the biscuits on a wire rack before adding the cats' features with melted chocolate (see page 17).

Step 4

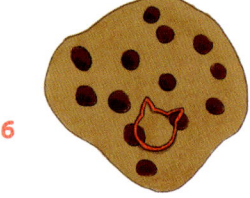

Step 6

Dango

Serves 5
Prep time: 20 minutes
Cooking time: 6 minutes

Ingredients
- 50g (1¾oz) rice flour
- 110g (4oz) glutinous rice flour
- 50g (1¾oz) caster sugar
- 1 teaspoon matcha green tea powder
- 90ml (3fl oz) hot water
- 2 drops of red food colouring

To decorate
- 1 fine black food-safe decorating pen

1 Mix both flours and the sugar together in a mixing bowl.

2 Dilute the matcha powder in 30ml (1fl oz) of the hot water in a bowl, then add one-third of the flour and sugar mixture. Mix to a soft but malleable consistency, adding a little extra water or flour if necessary. Shape into 5 small balls. Lightly flatten the top of 1 small ball to create ears, then press the ears between your thumb and index finger to give them a realistic shape. Repeat with the remaining balls.

3 Mix the red food colouring with 30ml (1fl oz) hot water in another bowl. Add half the remaining flour and sugar mixture.

4 Add the remaining 30ml (1fl oz) hot water to the mixing bowl containing the rest of the flour and sugar mixture.

5 Shape 10 cats' heads in the same way, 5 from each of the mixtures in the remaining bowls.

6 Bring a saucepan of water to the boil and add the balls to it in batches. When the balls float to the surface, cook them for a further 2 minutes. Drain them and then thread one of each colour ball on to 5 wooden skewers.

7 Draw on the cats' faces using a food-safe decorating pen (see page 17).

Step 2
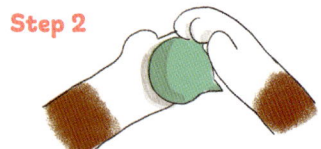

Step 6

Matcha

Although this powdered green tea is mainly served as a drink during the celebrated tea ceremony, matcha is also added to sweet recipes. Its extremely fine texture makes it easy to incorporate into mixtures for making desserts such as cakes, tiramisu, shortbread, ice creams and mochi, and its vibrant green colour and subtle flavour add a unique touch. This new star of contemporary sweet dishes is not just a treat for your eyes and taste buds but it also boasts health benefits!

Matcha latte

Makes 2 cups
Prep time: 15 minutes
Cooking time: 2 minutes

Ingredients

- 3 teaspoons matcha green tea powder
- 2 teaspoons icing sugar (or adjust according to personal taste)
- 50ml (2fl oz) hot water (about 80°C/176°F)
- 350ml (12fl oz) milk (or a non-dairy milk alternative of your choice)

Equipment

- electric milk frother or bamboo whisk

1 Sift the matcha powder into a large jug to remove any lumps and sift in the icing sugar. Pour in the hot water and mix with a milk frother (or use a traditional bamboo whisk) until the mixture is smooth.

2 Heat the milk to about 80°C (176°F), then create a mousse on top using the electric milk frother (or a bamboo whisk).

3 Divide the matcha between 2 cups, then carefully pour the milk mixture on top, reserving the mousse. Very gently spoon over the mousse using a teaspoon, shaping it into a cat's head and then adding the ears.

4 Add the eyes, muzzle, ear detail and whiskers, using matcha mixture carefully drawn from around the cat's head with the tip of a chopstick.

Step 3

Step 4

TIP

Adjust the amount of sugar that is added to suit your taste. Matcha latte can also be served cold in tall glasses. Add ice cubes before pouring in the milk base, followed by the matcha and water mixture.

110

Hot chocolate

Makes 2 cups
Prep time: 10 minutes
Cooking time: 2 minutes

Ingredients
- 80g (2¾oz) plain dark chocolate
- 400ml (14fl oz) milk (or a non-dairy milk alternative of your choice)
- 50ml (2fl oz) double cream (or a non-dairy cream alternative of your choice)
- 20g (¾oz) sugar
- 1 tablespoon unsweetened cocoa powder

Equipment
- electric milk frother or bamboo whisk

1 Break the chocolate into individual squares and place in a saucepan.

2 In another saucepan, heat the milk with the cream and the sugar. Remove the pan from the heat just before the milk and cream come to the boil.

3 Pour half of the milk and cream over the squares of chocolate and leave them to melt for 1 minute. Whisk until the mixture is smooth, before incorporating half of the remaining milk and cream.

4 Using an electric milk frother or bamboo whisk, froth the remaining half until it has reached a mousse-like consistency.

5 Divide the chocolate milk and cream between 2 cups, then very carefully spoon the milk foam over the chocolate mixture, reserving some of the foam to add on top at the end.

6 Holding a paw-shaped stencil above the mousse-like foam, dust over the cocoa powder.

Step 6

TIP
Use milk chocolate if preferred or increase the quantity of plain dark chocolate, depending on whether you like a drink with a milder or more pronounced chocolate flavour.

Glossary of UK/US Terms

UK	US
Baking parchment	Parchment paper
Beetroot	Beet
Caster sugar	Superfine sugar
Cornflour	Cornstarch
Clingfilm	Plastic wrap
Frying pan	Skillet
Ground almonds	Almond meal
Hand-held electric whisk	Electric beaters
Icing sugar	Confectioners' sugar
Kitchen paper	Paper towel
Minced pork/beef	Ground pork/beef
Plain dark chocolate	Semi-sweet chocolate
Plain flour	All-purpose flour
Spring onion	Scallion
Stock	Broth
Tea towel	Cloth kitchen towel
Vanilla pod	Vanilla bean

Where can I buy the equipment?

Online retailers

UK:
Japancentre.com
Souschef.co.uk

US:
Sayweee.com
Yami.com

Europe:
Asianfoodshop.eu
Irasshai.co
Nishikidori.com

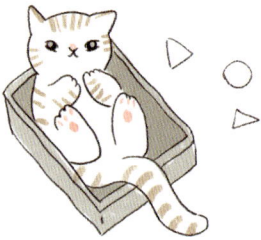

Index

A
allergies 125
anko (an) 13, 82, 84–5, 86
anpan meow 86–9
azuki bean paste 13, 82–5, 86

B
beef
    korokke croquettes 78
    soboro bento box 64
bento 40–3
bento box
    assembling 42–3
    soboro 64–5
biscuits/cookies
    cat tongue cookies 92–3
    meow meow biscuits 104–5
bookmark, origami cat 76–7
bread
    anpan meow 86–9
    burger buns 55–6
    sando 66–7
broccoli 42
buns, burger 55–6
burgers
    burger buns 55–6
    tonkatsu 54–7

C
cabbage 54, 60
carrot flowers 50, 64, 68
cat tongue cookies 92–3
cats, role in Japanese culture 7
cat's body, drawing 39
cat's face
    making 16–17
    onigiri 16, 32–3, 52–3
cat's head
    in bento box 42
    dango 106–7
    drawing 38
    mango mochi 90–1
    meow meow biscuits 104–5
    modelling 14–15, 32, 36, 47, 50
    onigiri 32–3, 52–3
    origami 76–7
cheese
    as garnish 16, 34, 42, 64
    vegetarian 125
chicken
    gyoza 61
    Japanese kare rice 52–3
    kara-age 40, 42
    tonkatsu burgers 54–7
chocolate
    cat tongue cookies 92
    hot 112–13
    making faces 87, 90, 94, 98, 101
    meow meow biscuits 104
    piping 17

colouring 28–31, 34
colours 18–19
cookies see biscuits/cookies
cream 90, 112
crème fraîche 98
croquettes, korokke 78–81
cucumber 47
cutters 9

D
dango 106–7
dashi 13
desserts 82
doughnuts 100–3
drawing
   cat's body 39
   cat's face 17
   cat's head 38
drinks
   hot chocolate 112–13
   matcha latte 110–11
dumplings, manju 72–5

E
eggs 125
   hard-boiled 52–3, 66
   in ice cream 98
   omelettes 22–5, 40–1, 42, 46
   sandwich 66–7
   scrambled 64
equipment 8–9, 118

G
glossary 116
gunkan 44
gyoza 58–63
   dough 62

H
ham 16, 34, 36, 64
hot chocolate 112–13

I
ice cream 96, 98–9
inari
   as garnish 42, 68
   inari zushi 50–1
   pockets 11, 13, 50, 68
ingredients 10–13

K
kare 13
kare rice 52–3
kitsuné udon 68–9
kittens 34–5
korokke croquettes 78–81

M

maki 44
mango mochi 90–1
manju dumplings 72–5
mascarpone cheese 90, 94
matcha 13, 108
   in dango 106
     latte 110–11
     tirami-cats 94–5
measurements 125
meow meow biscuits 104–5
milk 98, 110, 112, 125
miso 13
modelling tool 8
moulds
   for biscuits 93
   for rice 9

N

naruto 68–9
neko ice cream 98–9
nigiri 44
noodles, udon 13, 68–9
nori 12
   as colouring 18, 34
   as garnish 16, 32, 36, 64

O

oishi sushi 44
omelettes
   from egg whites 24–5
   from whole eggs 22–3, 36
   tamagoyaki 40–1, 42, 46
onigiri 16, 32–3, 52–3
origami cat 76–7
oven temperatures 125

P

panko 13, 78
patisserie, Japanese 82
paws 34–5, 36, 42, 52, 92, 113
pepper 125
piping bag 9, 17
pork
   gyoza 60
   manju dumplings 72–5
   soboro bento box 64–5
   tonkatsu burgers 54–7
potatoes, korokke croquettes 78
prawns
   as garnish 47
   gyoza 61
punches 8

R
ravioli, gyoza 58–63
rice
    Japanese 12
    kare 52–3
    kittens 32–3
    making onigiri 32
    moulds 9
    preparing 26–7, 46
    vinegar 12

S
salmon, cat sushi platter 46
sando 66–7
sandwich, egg 66–7
scalpel 8
scissors 8
sesame oil 12
sesame seeds 12
sleepyhead cat 36–7
soboro bento box 64–5
soup
    Japanese kare rice 52–3
    kitsuné udon 68–9
soy sauce 12
sponge fingers 94
stencils 8, 15
street food 70
    korokke croquettes 78–81
    manju dumplings 72–5

suppliers 118
sushi
    cat sushi platter 46–9
    different types 44
    inari zushi 50–1
sweet dishes 82

T
tea, green 13, 94, 106, 108
temaki 44
temari 44
tofu
    abure-age 50
    inari pockets 11, 50–1, 68
    kara-age 40
tonkatsu sauce 13
    burgers 54–7
korokke croquettes 78
tuna, cat sushi platter 46
tweezers 8

U
udon noodles 13
    kitsuné 68–9

V
vinegar, rice 12

Standard level spoon measurements are used in all recipes.
1 tablespoon = one 15ml spoon
1 teaspoon = one 5ml spoon

Both imperial and metric measurements have been given in all recipes. Use one set of measurements only and not a mixture of both.

Eggs should be medium unless otherwise stated. The Department of Health advises that eggs should not be consumed raw. This book contains dishes made with raw or lightly cooked eggs. It is prudent for more vulnerable people such as pregnant and nursing mothers, the elderly, babies and young children to avoid uncooked or lightly cooked dishes made with eggs. Once prepared these dishes should be kept refrigerated and used promptly.

Milk should be full fat unless otherwise stated.

Fresh herbs should be used unless otherwise stated. If unavailable use dried herbs as an alternative but halve the quantities stated.

Ovens should be preheated to the specific temperature – if using a fan-assisted oven, follow manufacturer's instructions for adjusting the time and the temperature.

Pepper should be freshly ground black pepper unless otherwise stated.

This book includes dishes made with nuts and nut derivatives. It is advisable for customers with known allergic reactions to nuts and nut derivatives and those who may be potentially vulnerable to these allergies, such as babies and children with a family history of allergies, to avoid dishes made with nuts and nut oils. It is also prudent to check the labels of pre-prepared ingredients for the possible inclusion of nut derivatives.

Vegetarians should look for the 'V' symbol on a cheese to ensure it is made with vegetarian rennet.

Acknowledgements

The idea for this book came about during a discussion one winter's day with my friend Haruna and my daughter Aya about our mutual fascination with cats. I never imagined that it would generate so much excitement around us.

My thanks go to Rennie for photographing the recipes so beautifully.

Thank you also to Aurélie and the entire Mango team for making the book so irresistible.

And, of course, I want to say a big thank you to Haruna, the book's talented illustrator.

Laure Kié

Published in France as Recettes Chatponaises by Mango Editions, 2025.

First published in Great Britain in 2026 by Mitchell Beazley, an imprint of Octopus Publishing Group Ltd
Carmelite House, 50 Victoria Embankment, London EC4Y 0DZ
www.octopusbooks.co.uk

An Hachette UK Company
www.hachette.co.uk

The authorized representative in the EEA is Hachette Ireland,
8 Castlecourt Centre, Dublin 15, D15 XTP3, Ireland (email: info@hbgi.ie)

This edition 2026.

Copyright © Mango Editions, Paris, 2025
English translation copyright © Octopus Publishing Group Ltd 2026

Distributed in the US by Hachette Book Group
1290 Avenue of the Americas, 4th and 5th Floors, New York, NY 10104

Distributed in Canada by Canadian Manda Group
664 Annette St., Toronto, Ontario, Canada M6S 2C8

All rights reserved. No part of this work may be reproduced or utilized in any form or by any means, electronic or mechanical, including photocopying, recording or by any information storage and retrieval system, without the prior written permission of the publisher.

ISBN: 978-1-84601-667-7
eISBN: 978-1-84601-692-9

A CIP catalogue record for this book is available from the British Library.

Printed and bound in China.

1 3 5 7 9 10 8 6 4 2

French edition:
Recipes and text: Laure Kié

Photographer: Rennie Triana
Illustrator: Haruna Kishi
Publishing Director: Guillaume Pô
Editorial Director: Tatiana Delesalle
Editor: Aurélie Cazenave assisted by Salomé Leger-Pereira
Art Director: Chloé Eve
Layout: Julie Bureau

English edition:
Commissioning Editor: Jeannie Stanley
Editor: Scarlet Furness
Translators: Wendy Sweetser, Jane Moseley and Jackie Strachan
Copy Editor: Vicky Orchard
Creative Director: Jonathan Christie
Senior Production Manager: Peter Hunt

MIX
Paper | Supporting responsible forestry
FSC® C016973